50 Paleo
Soups and Stews

Table of Contents

Introduction

If you are following the Paleo diet, you may find it challenging to find healthy recipes that follow the guidelines of the Paleo diet. In this book you will find a wide assortment of soups and stews that are made only with Paleo-friendly ingredients. You no longer have to worry about making substitutions or experimenting with complicated recipes. From classics like chicken vegetable soup and butternut squash soup to unique flavors like Asian beef with vegetables and curried lamb stew, the recipes in this book are sure to please!

Poultry Recipes

Mexican Chicken Stew

Prep Time: 45 minutes

Servings: 6

Ingredients:

- 3 ½ cups chicken stock
- 3 cups cooked chicken, shredded
- 1 (28 oz.) can diced tomatoes
- 3 tbsp. olive oil
- 1 tbsp. minced garlic
- 1 onion, chopped
- 2 jalapeno peppers, seeded and minced
- 1 tbsp. dried oregano

- 1 tsp. cumin
- ½ tsp. chili powder
- Juice from 1 lime
- Fresh chopped cilantro

Instructions:

Heat the oil in a large saucepan over medium heat. Add the onion and cook for 2 minutes. Stir in the garlic and jalapeno and cook until translucent, about 3 minutes. Add the spices and cook for 1 minute more then stir in the tomatoes, chicken and chicken stock. Bring to a simmer and cook for 20 minutes, stirring occasionally. Squeeze the lime into the pot and cook for 5 minutes more. Ladle into bowls and garnish with fresh chopped cilantro.

Chicken Vegetable Soup

Prep Time: 45 minutes

Servings: 4 to 6

Ingredients:

- 1 lbs. boneless skinless chicken breasts
- 2 tbsp. coconut oil
- 2 cloves garlic, minced
- 1 onion, chopped
- 2 cups chopped carrots
- 1 cup sliced celery
- 4 cups water
- 1 ½ cups chicken broth
- ¼ cup fresh chopped parsley
- Sea salt and pepper to taste

9

Instructions:

Place the water and chicken broth in a saucepan and bring to a simmer. Add the chicken and simmer for 5 to 6 minutes. Remove from heat and cover. Let stand for 15 minutes until the chicken is cooked through then remove it to a cutting board, reserving the water. Heat the oil in a Dutch oven over medium heat. Add the onion and cook until softened, about 5 minutes. Stir in the garlic and cook for 1 minute more. Add the carrots, celery, sea salt and pepper then cook, covered, for 8 to 10 minutes. Stir in the water from the chicken and bring to a simmer. Simmer for 8 to 10 minutes until the vegetables are tender then remove from heat. Shred the chicken and stir it into the soup with the parsley. Serve hot.

Chicken Stock

Prep Time: 7 ½ hours

Servings: 1 gallon

Ingredients:

- 4 lbs. chicken carcass
- 1 tbsp. coconut oil
- 1 tsp. minced garlic
- 1 large onion, quartered
- 3 carrots, cut in half
- 3 stalks celery, cut in half
- ½ bunch fresh thyme
- ½ bunch fresh parsley
- 2 bay leaves
- 1 tsp. sea salt

- Water as needed

Instructions:

Heat the coconut oil in a large stockpot over medium heat. Add the garlic, onions, carrots and celery and cook until tender, about 5 to 10 minutes. Place the chicken carcass in the stockpot and top with thyme, parsley, bay leaves and salt. Fill the pot with enough water to cover the chicken carcass and bring to a boil. Reduce heat and simmer, uncovered, for 6 to 7 hours. Use a mesh strainer to skim the fat off the top of the liquid every 20 to 30 minutes. Strain the stock through a mesh sieve and discard the solids. Use the stock in your favorite Paleo soups and stews as needed.

White Chicken Chili

Prep Time: 45 minutes

Servings: 6

Ingredients:

- 4 cups cooked chicken, chopped
- 4 cups chicken stock
- 1 tbsp. coconut oil
- 1 tsp. minced garlic
- 2 cups finely chopped cauliflower
- 1 onion, chopped
- 1 tsp. dried oregano
- 1 tsp. cumin
- Dash cayenne pepper
- Chopped green onions

Instructions:

Heat the coconut oil in a stockpot over medium-high heat. Stir in the onion and cook until tender, about 5 minutes. Add the spices and cook for another 5 minutes, stirring occasionally. Stir in the chopped cauliflower and bring the mixture to a gentle simmer. Cook for 20 to 25 minutes, stirring occasionally. Stir in the chicken and cook for 5 minutes or until heated through. Serve hot garnished with green onions.

Curried Turkey with Onion Soup

Prep Time: 1 hour

Servings: 4 to 6

Ingredients:

- 3 cups cooked turkey, chopped
- 2 cups chopped onion
- 10 oz. baby spinach
- 1 ½ cups diced sweet potato
- 1 cup chopped carrot
- ½ cup chopped celery
- 2 tbsp. coconut oil
- 3 tbsp. almond flour
- 2 tsp. curry powder

- 2 (14.5 oz.) cans chicken broth
- 2 cups coconut milk
- Sea salt and pepper to taste
- Fresh chopped parsley

Instructions:

Wash the baby spinach and pat the leaves dry. Melt the coconut oil in a Dutch oven over medium heat. Stir in the onion and cook until tender, about 5 to 7 minutes. Add the curry powder and almond flour, whisking the mixture smooth. Cook for 3 minutes while constantly whisking. Whisk in the broth in a steady stream then add the sweet potato, carrots and celery. Bring the mixture to a boil and cook until it begins to thicken. Reduce heat and simmer, covered, for 15 minutes. Stir in the turkey, spinach, coconut milk, sea salt and pepper. Cover and simmer 10 minutes more then serve hot garnished with fresh parsley.

Turkey with Red Cabbage Soup

Prep Time: 40 minutes

Servings: 10

Ingredients:

- 1 lbs. lean ground turkey
- 1 tbsp. coconut oil
- 2 onions, chopped
- 1 head red cabbage, chopped
- 3 sweet potatoes, chopped
- 1 cup chopped carrots
- 1 tbsp. cold water
- 2 tsp. tapioca starch
- 1 (49.5 oz.) can chicken broth
- Sea salt and pepper to taste

17

Instructions:

Heat the oil in a stockpot over medium heat and add the turkey and onions. Cook until the turkey is browned then drain the fat. Stir in the sweet potato, cabbage, carrots and chicken broth. Season with salt and pepper to taste and bring to a boil. Reduce heat and simmer, covered, for 20 minutes or until the sweet potatoes are tender. Whisk together the water and tapioca starch then drizzle into the soup. Bring to a boil and cook for 2 minutes until thickened. Serve hot.

Easy Chicken Stew

Prep Time: 1 hour

Servings: 8 to 10

Ingredients:

- 2 lbs. chicken, chopped
- 1 lbs. chopped carrots
- 8 oz. sliced mushrooms
- 2 cups chopped onion
- 2 cups chopped sweet potato
- ½ cup almond flour
- 1 tbsp. coconut oil
- 3 cloves garlic, minced
- 1 (14 oz.) can low-sodium chicken stock
- 1 ½ tsp. dried thyme

- Sea salt and pepper to taste

Instructions:

Season the chicken with sea salt and pepper to taste then set aside. Heat the coconut oil in a Dutch oven over medium-high heat and add the chicken. Cook until lightly browned, about 5 minutes. Spoon the chicken into a bowl and reduce the heat. Add the garlic, onions and sweet potatoes and cook for 3 to 4 minutes, stirring. Pour the chicken stock into the Dutch oven and stir to scrape up the browned bits on the bottom of the skillet. Stir in the dried thyme then add the rest of the ingredients, including the chicken. Cover and simmer for 30 to 40 minutes until the vegetables are tender and the mixture is heated through. Serve hot.

Spicy Chicken Vegetable Stew

Prep Time: 1 hour

Servings: 8 to 10

Ingredients:

- 2 lbs. chicken, chopped
- 2 cups chopped carrots
- 2 cups broccoli florets
- 2 cups chopped onion
- 1 cup chopped sweet potato
- 1 cup sliced mushrooms
- 1 tbsp. coconut oil
- 1 jalapeno pepper, seeded and minced
- 3 cloves garlic, minced
- ½ cup almond flour

- 1 (14 oz.) can low-sodium chicken stock

- 1 ½ tsp. dried oregano

- ½ tsp. cayenne pepper

- Sea salt and pepper to taste

Instructions:

Season the chicken with sea salt and pepper to taste then set aside. Heat the coconut oil in a Dutch oven over medium-high heat and add the chicken. Cook until lightly browned, about 5 minutes. Spoon the chicken into a bowl and reduce the heat. Add the garlic, jalapeno, onions and mushrooms and cook for 3 to 4 minutes, stirring. Pour the chicken stock into the Dutch oven and stir to scrape up the browned bits on the bottom of the skillet. Stir in the dried oregano and cayenne pepper then add the rest of the ingredients, including the chicken. Cover and simmer for 30 to 40 minutes until the vegetables are tender and the mixture is heated through. Serve hot.

Fire-Roasted Tomato Chicken Soup

Prep Time: 1 hour

Servings: 4 to 6

Ingredients:

- 10 large tomatoes, cored and halved
- 1 large onion, sliced thin
- 1 tbsp. minced garlic
- 2 tbsp. olive oil
- 1 cup chicken stock
- ½ cup fresh basil, chopped
- ½ cup coconut milk
- 2 cups cooked chicken, shredded
- Sea salt and pepper to taste

Instructions:

Preheat the oven to 375°F. Spread the tomatoes and onion on a baking sheet and top with garlic and chopped basil. Drizzle the olive oil over top and bake for 45 minutes, stirring halfway through. Spoon the vegetables into a stockpot then stir in the broth. Bring to a boil then remove from heat and blend using an immersion blender. Return to the heat and stir in the coconut milk and chicken. Season with sea salt and pepper to taste and cook until heated through.

Mediterranean Chicken Stew

Prep Time: 1 hour

Servings: 8 to 10

Ingredients:

- 2 lbs. chicken, chopped
- 2 cups chopped onion
- 1 cup chopped carrots
- 1 cup chopped tomatoes
- 8 oz. sliced mushrooms
- ½ cup almond flour
- 1 tbsp. coconut oil
- 1 tbsp. minced garlic
- 1 tsp. dried thyme
- ½ tsp. dried rosemary

- 1 cup sliced kalamata olives
- 1 (14 oz.) can low-sodium chicken stock
- Sea salt and pepper to taste

Instructions:

Season the chicken with sea salt and pepper to taste then set aside. Heat the coconut oil in a Dutch oven over medium-high heat and add the chicken. Cook until lightly browned, about 5 minutes. Spoon the chicken into a bowl and reduce the heat. Add the garlic, onions and carrots and cook for 3 to 4 minutes, stirring. Pour the chicken stock into the Dutch oven and stir to scrape up the browned bits on the bottom of the skillet. Stir in the dried thyme and rosemary then add the rest of the ingredients, including the chicken. Cover and simmer for 30 to 40 minutes until the vegetables are tender and the mixture is heated through. Serve hot.

Beef Recipes

Spicy Red Chili

Prep Time: 2 to 4 hours

Servings: 4 to 6

Ingredients:

- 2 lbs. lean ground beef
- 3 ½ cups organic diced tomatoes
- 1 tbsp. coconut oil
- 1 tsp. minced garlic
- 1 onion, diced
- 1 red pepper, diced
- 2 tbsp. chili powder
- 1 tbsp. cumin

- ½ tsp. cayenne
- Water as needed

Instructions:

Heat the oil in a large stockpot over medium heat. Add the ground beef and cook until browned then drain the fat. Stir in the garlic, onion and red pepper. Cook for 5 to 8 minutes until the vegetables are tender. Stir in the spices and cook 1 minute more. Add the remaining ingredients and fill the pot with enough water to cover the ingredients. Reduce heat and simmer, covered, for 2 to 4 hours until heated through.

Asian Beef Soup

Prep Time: 1 ½ hours

Servings: 4 to 6

Ingredients:

- 1 ½ lbs. beef sirloin, chopped
- 1 tbsp. coconut oil
- 4 stalks celery, chopped
- 2 carrots, chopped
- 1 onion, chopped
- 1 cup diced tomatoes
- 1 can water chestnuts, drained
- ¼ cup fresh parsley, chopped
- 1 tbsp. coconut aminos

- 2 tsp. sesame oil
- 1 tsp. fresh grated ginger
- 1 tsp. minced garlic
- 8 cups beef stock

Instructions:

Heat the oil in a large stockpot over medium heat and stir in the chopped beef sirloin. Cook until browned on all sides then scoop out using a slotted spoon. Add the ginger and garlic and cook for 1 minute. Stir in the carrots, celery and onions and cook for 5 to 10 minutes until tender. Stir in the remaining ingredients and add the beef back to the pot. Bring to a boil then reduce heat and simmer, covered, for about 45 minutes or until the beef is tender.

Easy Beef Stew

Prep Time: 1 hour

Servings: 4 to 6

Ingredients:

- 2 lbs. stew beef
- 1 tbsp. minced garlic
- 1 tbsp. coconut oil
- 1 large onion, quartered
- 2 cups chopped carrots
- 1 cup diced tomatoes
- 1 cup beef stock
- 2 tsp. dried basil
- 1 tsp. dried oregano
- Salt and pepper to taste

Instructions:

Heat the oil and garlic in a stockpot over medium heat. Season the beef with sea salt and pepper then add to the pot. Cook until browned on all sides, about 5 minutes. Scoop out the beef using a slotted spoon and add the onion and carrots to the stockpot. Cook for 10 minutes until tender. Stir in the remaining ingredients and add the beef back to the pot. Reduce heat and simmer, covered, for 20 to 30 minutes until heated through.

Beef with Wild Mushroom Soup

Prep Time: 2 hours

Servings: 4 to 6

Ingredients:

- 1 lbs. stew beef
- 8 oz. sliced wild mushrooms
- 1 tbsp. coconut oil
- 2 tsp. minced garlic
- 1 onion, chopped
- 2 tbsp. tomato paste
- 1 cup dry red wine
- 8 cups beef broth
- 1 tsp. dried sage
- ½ tsp. dried oregano

- ¼ cup coconut milk

Instructions:

Heat the oil in a large stockpot over medium heat. Add the garlic, mushrooms and onion and cook until tender, about 5 minutes. Scoop the vegetables out of the pot and raise the heat. Cook the meat on medium-high heat until browned on all sides. Whisk in the tomato paste and add the vegetables back to the pot. Stir in the remaining ingredients aside from the coconut milk and bring to a boil. Reduce heat and simmer, covered, for 1 ½ hours, stirring occasionally. Remove from heat and stir in the coconut milk. Serve hot.

Beef Stew with Caramelized Onions

Prep Time: 1 hour 30 minutes

Servings: 6

Ingredients:

- 1 ½ lbs. stew beef
- 1 tbsp. coconut oil
- 1 tsp. minced garlic
- 4 cups sliced onions
- 2 cups chopped carrots
- 1 cup chopped parsnips
- 1 cup beef broth
- 2 tsp. fresh chopped thyme
- Sea salt and pepper to taste

Instructions:

Heat the oil and garlic in a stockpot over medium heat. Season the beef with sea salt and pepper and set aside. Add the onions to the stockpot and cook for 30 to 35 minutes until caramelized. Stir in the thyme and beef and cook for 5 minutes or until lightly browned. Stir in the remaining ingredients and bring to a boil. Reduce heat and simmer, covered, for 30 to 45 minutes until the beef is cooked through.

Greek-Style Beef Stew

Prep Time: 1 hour

Servings: 4 to 6

Ingredients:

- 2 ½ lbs. stew beef
- 2 tbsp. olive oil
- 2 tbsp. minced garlic
- 1 onion, chopped
- 1 cup diced tomatoes
- ½ cup kalamata olives, sliced
- ½ cup beef stock
- 2 bay leaves
- 1 tsp. dried thyme
- Salt and pepper to taste

Instructions:

Heat the oil and garlic in a stockpot over medium heat. Season the beef with sea salt and pepper then add to the pot. Cook until browned on all sides, about 5 minutes. Scoop out the beef using a slotted spoon and add the onion to the stockpot. Cook for 10 minutes until tender. Stir in the remaining ingredients and add the beef back to the pot. Reduce heat and simmer, covered, for 20 to 30 minutes until heated through.

Beef Stock

Prep Time: 6 hours

Servings: 1 gallon

Ingredients:

- 4 lbs. beef bones
- 1 tbsp. coconut oil
- 3 cloves garlic, peeled
- 1 large onion, quartered
- 2 large carrots, halved
- 2 stalks celery, halved
- 2 bay leaves
- 1 tbsp. whole peppercorns
- ½ bunch fresh parsley
- Water as needed

Instructions:

Heat the coconut oil in a large stockpot over medium heat. Stir in the onion, carrot and celery and cook until tender, about 10 minutes. Add the beef bones and top with bay leaves, peppercorns and parsley. Fill the pot with enough water to just cover the ingredients. Bring to a boil then reduce heat and simmer for about 5 hours. Strain the stock through a mesh sieve and discard the solids.

Creamy Beef Stroganoff

Prep Time: 45 minutes

Servings: 4

Ingredients:

- 1 lbs. beef sirloin, sliced
- 6 tbsp. coconut oil, divided
- 1 tsp. minced garlic
- 8 oz. sliced mushroom
- 1 onion, chopped
- 1 cup beef stock
- 1 cup coconut milk
- ¼ cup dry white wine
- Sea salt and pepper to taste

Instructions:

Heat a large skillet over medium heat and add 2 tbsp. coconut oil. Add the beef and cook on each side for about 1 minute or until lightly browned. Scoop the beef out of the skillet and add 2 more tbsp. coconut oil. Add the mushrooms and cook for about 5 minutes then scoop them out of the skillet. Add the onions and garlic, cooking for about 10 minutes until tender. Stir in the white wine and cook until the wine cooks off. Whisk in the coconut milk and beef broth, stirring until slightly thickened. Add the remaining ingredients and bring to a simmer. Cook for 5 to 7 minutes and serve hot.

Spicy Taco Soup

Prep Time: 1 hour

Servings: 4

Ingredients:

- 1 lbs. lean ground beef
- 1 tsp. coconut oil
- 1 tbsp. minced garlic
- 4 diced tomatoes
- 1 red onion, chopped
- 1 (4 oz.) can roasted green chiles
- 1 cup fresh salsa
- 2 cups chicken stock
- 1 tbsp. chili powder

- ¼ tsp. garlic powder
- ¼ tsp. crushed red pepper flakes
- Dash cayenne pepper

Instructions:

Heat the oil in a stockpot over medium heat and add the beef. Cook until browned then drain the fat and scoop the meat out into a bowl. Add the garlic and cook for 1 minute. Stir in the onion and chiles and cook for 5 to 7 minutes until translucent. Stir in the remaining ingredients and bring to a boil. Reduce heat and simmer, covered, for 35 to 45 minutes until the vegetables are tender.

Corned Beef with Cabbage Soup

Prep Time: 45 minutes

Servings: 4

Ingredients:

- ¼ lbs. corned beef, sliced thin
- 2 tbsp. coconut oil
- 3 large tomatoes, halved
- 1 onion, roughly chopped
- 1 cup chopped carrot
- 1 cup chopped celery
- 4 cups chopped green cabbage
- 2 ½ cups beef stock
- ¼ tsp. ground allspice

Instructions:

Combine the onion, celery and carrots in a food processor and pulse until finely chopped. Heat the oil in a stockpot over medium heat and stir in the chopped vegetables and allspice. Cook until softened, about 5 minutes. Chop the tomatoes in the food processor and add them to the pot along with the broth, cabbage and 4 cups of water. Bring to a boil then reduce heat and simmer, uncovered, for about 20 minutes. Stir in the corned beef and cook until heated through.

Pork and Lamb Recipes

Asian Pork with Mushroom Soup

Prep Time: 20 minutes

Servings: 6

Ingredients:

- 12 oz. boneless pork, chopped
- 1 tsp. coconut oil
- 2 tsp. minced garlic
- 2 cups sliced mushrooms
- 2 cups chopped Chinese cabbage
- 3 (14.5 oz.) cans chicken broth
- 2 tbsp. dry white wine
- 2 tbsp. coconut aminos

- ½ tsp. ground ginger
- ¼ tsp. red pepper flakes
- 1 green onion, chopped

Instructions:

Heat the oil in a saucepan over medium heat. Add the pork and cook for 2 to 3 minutes or until lightly browned. Spoon the pork into a bowl and add the mushrooms and garlic to the pot. Cook until tender, about 5 minutes. Stir in the chicken broth, wine, coconut aminos, ginger and pepper flakes. Bring to a boil then stir in the pork and cabbage. Heat through then serve garnished with green onion.

Curried Lamb Stew

Prep Time: 1 hour

Servings: 6 to 8

Ingredients:

- 2 lbs. boneless lamb shoulder
- 4 sweet potatoes, cut into 1-inch chunks
- 1 tbsp. coconut oil
- 1 tbsp. minced garlic
- 1 onion, quartered
- 1 cup diced tomatoes
- 1 cup water
- 1 tbsp. curry powder
- 1 tsp. cumin
- 1 tsp. turmeric

- 1/8 tsp. cayenne
- Salt and pepper to taste

Instructions:

Heat the olive oil in a Dutch oven over medium heat. Add the garlic and spices and cook for 1 minute. Stir in the lamb then cook until browned on all sides then spoon out into a bowl. Add the onions and cook for 5 minutes then stir in the tomatoes and cook for 1 minute more. Stir in the remaining ingredients and bring to a boil. Reduce heat and simmer, covered, for 35 minutes or until the vegetables are tender. Serve hot.

Sausage with Red Pepper Soup

Prep Time: 25 minutes

Servings: 4

Ingredients:

- 4 cooked sausage links, chopped
- 4 roasted red peppers, chopped
- 2 tbsp. coconut oil
- 1 tbsp. minced garlic
- 1 avocado, pitted and chopped
- 1 onion, diced
- 1 cup vegetable stock
- 1 cup canned coconut milk
- 1 tbsp. smoked paprika
- 1 tbsp. paprika

- 1 tsp. red pepper flakes
- Chopped cilantro leaves

Instructions:

Heat the coconut oil and garlic in a saucepan over medium heat. Add the onions and cook until translucent, about 6 minutes. Stir in the roasted red peppers, broth, coconut milk and spices. Simmer for 8 to 10 minutes. Add the avocado and blend the soup using an immersion blender. Spoon the soup into bowls and top with sausage and chopped cilantro.

Tuscan Lamb and Vegetable Stew

Prep Time: 2 hours

Servings: 6

Ingredients:

- 3 lbs. boneless leg of lamb, chopped
- 3 tbsp. olive oil
- 1 tbsp. minced garlic
- 3 ½ cups beef broth
- 1 ½ cups red wine
- 1 (15 oz.) can diced tomatoes
- 1 chopped onion
- 2 tbsp. almond flour
- 1 tbsp. tomato paste
- 2 large carrots, chopped

- 2 stalks celery, chopped
- Sea salt and pepper to taste

Instructions:

Heat the oil in a Dutch oven over medium heat. Toss the lamb in the almond flour and season with salt and pepper to taste. Add the lamb to the pot and cook until browned, about 10 minutes. Spoon the lamb into a bowl and drain the fat. Add the garlic to the Dutch oven and cook for 1 minute before stirring in the wine. Reduce heat and stir, cooking for 5 minutes until the wine cooks off. Return the lamb to the pot along with the tomatoes, broth and tomato paste. Simmer, partially covered, for 1 hour or until the lamb is tender. Add the onions, carrots and celery to the stew and simmer for 25 minutes more.

Spiced Pumpkin Lamb Stew

Prep Time: 35 minutes

Servings: 2 to 4

Ingredients:

- 1 lbs. chopped lamb
- 1 tbsp. coconut oil
- 1 tbsp. olive oil
- 2 small pumpkins, peeled seeded and chopped
- 1 onion, chopped
- ¼ cup water
- 3 tbsp. tomato paste
- 1 tsp. turmeric
- Pinch ground cinnamon
- Sea salt and pepper to taste

Instructions:

Heat the coconut oil in a stockpot over medium heat. Season the lamb with salt and pepper then add to the pot and brown on all sides. Stir in 1 ½ cups water, tomato paste, turmeric and cinnamon. Add the onion and simmer for 1 ½ hours. Heat the olive oil in a skillet over medium heat and add the pumpkin. Cook until lightly browned then stir into the stockpot. Simmer, covered, for 20 minutes or until the pumpkin is tender. Serve hot.

Spicy Sausage Stew

Prep Time: 3 hours

Servings: 10 to 12

Ingredients:

- 2 lbs. pork shoulder, chopped
- 1 ½ lbs. hot Italian sausage links, sliced
- 1 tbsp. olive oil
- 1 onion, chopped
- 1 carrot, chopped
- 2 ½ cups water
- 1 (15 oz.) can crushed tomatoes
- 2 tbsp. paprika
- 1 tsp. smoked paprika
- 1 tsp. cayenne pepper

- 1 cup chopped parsley

Instructions:

Heat the oil in a stockpot over medium heat. Add the pork and cook until lightly browned then spoon into a bowl. Drain off most of the fat then stir in the chopped onion and carrot. Cook until tender then stir in the garlic and cook 1 minute more. Add the pork, sausage, crushed tomatoes and water then stir well. Season with paprika, smoked paprika and cayenne then bring to a simmer. Simmer for at least 2 hours until the pork is tender. Stir in the parsley and cook for 5 minutes before serving.

Pork and Vegetable Stew

Prep Time: 1 hour

Servings: 6 to 8

Ingredients:

- 2 lbs. boneless pork shoulder, cut into chunks
- 4 sweet potatoes, chopped
- 1 tbsp. coconut oil
- 1 tbsp. minced garlic
- 1 cup diced tomatoes
- 1 onion, quartered
- 1 cup water
- 1 tbsp. chili powder
- 1 tsp. cumin
- 1 tsp. dried oregano

- Salt and pepper to taste

Instructions:

Heat the olive oil in a Dutch oven over medium heat. Add the garlic and spices and cook for 1 minute. Stir in the pork then cook until browned on all sides then spoon out into a bowl. Add the onions and cook for 5 minutes then stir in the tomatoes and cook for 1 minute more. Stir in the remaining ingredients and bring to a boil. Reduce heat and simmer, covered, for 35 minutes or until the vegetables are tender. Serve hot.

Lamb Curry Soup

Prep Time: 1 hour

Servings: 4 to 6

Ingredients:

- 3 cups cooked lamb, chopped
- 2 tbsp. coconut oil
- 3 tbsp. almond flour
- 2 tsp. curry powder
- 2 cups chopped onion
- 1 ½ cups diced sweet potato
- 1 cup chopped carrot
- ½ cup chopped celery
- 2 (14.5 oz.) cans beef broth
- 2 cups coconut milk

- Sea salt and pepper to taste
- Fresh chopped parsley

Instructions:

Heat the coconut oil in a large stockpot over medium heat. Stir in the onion and cook until tender, about 5 to 7 minutes. Add the curry powder and almond flour, whisking the mixture smooth. Cook for 3 minutes while constantly whisking. Whisk in the broth in a steady stream then add the sweet potato, carrots and celery. Bring the mixture to a boil and cook until it begins to thicken. Reduce heat and simmer, covered, for 15 minutes. Stir in the lamb, coconut milk, sea salt and pepper. Cover and simmer 10 minutes more then serve hot garnished with fresh parsley.

Pork with Fajita Vegetable Soup

Prep Time: 1 hour

Servings: 4

Ingredients:

- 1 lbs. pork shoulder, cut into chunks
- 1 tbsp. coconut oil
- 1 tbsp. minced garlic
- 1 cup diced tomatoes
- 1 onion, chopped
- 1 red pepper, chopped
- 1 green pepper, chopped
- 1 (4 oz.) can roasted green chiles
- 2 cups chicken stock
- 1 tbsp. chili powder

- ¼ tsp. garlic powder
- ¼ tsp. crushed red pepper flakes

Instructions:

Heat the oil in a Dutch oven over medium heat and add the pork Cook until browned then drain the fat and scoop the meat out into a bowl. Add the garlic and cook for 1 minute. Stir in the onion, peppers and chiles and cook for 5 to 7 minutes until translucent. Stir in the remaining ingredients and bring to a boil. Reduce heat and simmer, covered, for 35 to 45 minutes until the vegetables are tender.

Split Pea Soup

Prep Time: 2 ½ hours

Servings: 4

Ingredients:

- 2 ½ cups dried split peas
- 1½ lbs. ham, bone-in
- 1 onion, chopped
- 1 cup diced carrots
- 1 cup diced celery
- ½ tsp. salt
- ¼ tsp. black pepper
- 8 cups water

Instructions:

Soak the split peas in water overnight in a large stockpot. Bring the stockpot to boil after adding the ham, onion, salt and pepper. Reduce heat and simmer, covered, for 1 ½ hours. Stir several times. Remove the ham bone and cut the meat off the bone. Dice the ham and stir it back into the pot. Stir in the rest of the ingredients and simmer, uncovered, for 30 minutes or until the vegetables are tender.

Seafood Recipes

Spicy Fish Stew

Prep Time: 25 minutes

Servings: 6

Ingredients:

- 2 lbs. cod fillets, cut into chunks
- ¼ cup olive oil
- 3 red peppers, chopped
- 2 (14.5 oz.) cans chopped tomatoes
- 1 cup chopped green onion
- ½ cup chopped cilantro
- 2 tsp. minced garlic
- 1 tsp. lemon zest

- ¾ tsp. red pepper flakes

Instructions:

Heat the oil in a large skillet over medium heat and stir in the green onions. Cool until tender, about 3 minutes. Stir in the peppers, tomatoes, garlic and red pepper flakes. Simmer for 10 minutes then stir in the cilantro, lemon zest and fish. Simmer until the fish is just opaque, about 5 minutes. Spoon into bowls to serve.

Asian-Style Seafood Soup

Prep Time: 35 minutes

Servings: 6

Ingredients:

- 1 lbs. red snapper fillet
- ½ lbs. raw shrimp, peeled and deveined
- 1 cup sliced mushrooms
- 2 shredded carrots
- 3 cups water
- 3 cups clam juice
- 4 scallions, sliced
- 2 stalks lemongrass, minced
- 2 tbsp. minced ginger
- 1 tsp. minced garlic

- 1 tbsp. fish sauce
- 1 cup chopped cilantro

Instructions:

Boil the water and clam juice in a stockpot over high heat. Stir in the scallions, ginger, lemongrass and garlic. Reduce heat and simmer for 10 minutes then stir in the fish sauce. Cut the fish into large chunks and add to the pot along with the shrimp, mushrooms and carrots. Cook over medium heat until the fish and shrimp are opaque, about 4 to 5 minutes. Discard the lemon grass and stir in the cilantro to serve.

Shrimp and Scallop Stew

Prep Time: 30 minutes

Servings: 4

Ingredients:

- ¾ lbs. raw shrimp, peeled and deveined
- ¾ lbs. raw sea scallops
- 2 tbsp. olive oil
- 2 chopped leeks, white and light green parts only
- 1 ½ cups chopped tomatoes
- 1 carrot, diced
- 3 cloves garlic, minced
- 1 cup dry white wine
- 1 tsp. ground cumin
- ¼ tsp. cayenne pepper

- ¼ cup fresh chopped cilantro

Instructions:

Heat the oil in a stockpot over medium heat. Add the leeks and garlic and cook until translucent, about 8 minutes. Stir in the carrots and spices then reduce heat and cook for 5 minutes. Stir in the tomatoes, white wine and 1 cup water then bring to a boil. Reduce heat and simmer for 5 minutes. Stir in the shrimp and scallops and cook until opaque, about 4 to 6 minutes. Remove from heat and stir in the cilantro to serve.

Sweet and Sour Scallop Soup

Prep Time: 1 hour

Servings: 4 to 6

Ingredients:

- 2 lbs. raw sea scallops
- 2 tbsp. olive oil
- 2 tbsp. coconut oil
- 2 cups sliced mushrooms
- ½ cup bamboo shoots
- ½ cup chopped green onion
- 4 large eggs, beaten
- 8 cups chicken stock
- ½ cup water
- 1/3 cup tapioca starch

- ¼ cup coconut aminos
- ¼ cup rice wine vinegar
- 1 tbsp. sesame oil

Instructions:

Heat the olive oil in a wok over medium heat. Add the mushrooms and bamboo shoots and cook for 2 minutes. Stir in the stock and bring to a boil then reduce heat and simmer for 5 minutes. Whisk together the tapioca starch and water then stir into the simmering soup. Bring to a boil and cook for 3 minutes. Reduce heat again and simmer while stirring in the coconut aminos and rice wine vinegar. Drizzle in the beaten eggs and stir gently until they are cooked through. Stir in the green onions. In a separate skillet over high heat, heat the coconut oil. Add the scallops and cook for 30 seconds on each side. Spoon the scallops into bowls and ladle the soup over them.

Ginger Shrimp and Scallops Soup

Prep Time: 20 minutes

Servings: 2

Ingredients:

- ¼ lbs. uncooked shrimp
- ¼ lbs. raw scallops
- 2 Portobello mushrooms, sliced
- 1 cup sliced shitake mushrooms
- ½ cup sliced ginger root
- ½ cup chopped green onion
- ¼ cup chopped cilantro

Instructions:

Bring the stock to a boil in a saucepan and add the ginger.

Simmer for 5 minutes then scoop the ginger out of the stock. Add the mushrooms and cook for 5 minutes then stir in the shrimp and simmer for 1 minute more. Stir in the scallops and cook for 1 minute then remove from heat. Stir in the cilantro and chopped green onions just before serving.

Shrimp and Sausage Stew

Prep Time: 30 minutes

Servings: 6 to 8

Ingredients:

- 3 tbsp. olive oil
- 2 lbs. shell-on shrimp, raw
- 1 lbs. Andouille sausage, sliced
- 2 cups chopped tomatoes
- 1 onion, chopped
- 1 stalk celery, chopped
- ½ red pepper, chopped
- 1 tbsp. minced garlic
- 1 cup chicken stock

- ¼ cup chopped parsley
- ¼ tsp. cayenne pepper

Instructions:

Heat the oil in a large, deep skillet and add the sausage. Cook for 5 minutes or until lightly browned then spoon out onto a plate. Stir in the onion, celery and red pepper and cook until softened, about 5 minutes. Stir in the garlic and cayenne and cook for 1 minute. Add the tomatoes and cook for 5 minutes then add the stock and bring to a boil. Return the sausage to the skillet and add the shrimp and half the parsley. Cover and simmer for 15 minutes or until the shrimp are cooked through. Let sit for 5 minutes then serve with remaining parsley.

Cajun Fish with Peppers Stew

Prep Time: 35 minutes

Servings: 2

Ingredients:

- 10 oz. halibut, cut into 1-inch chunks
- 1 tbsp. coconut oil
- 1 tsp. minced garlic
- ½ cup chopped red onion
- 1 (12 oz.) jar roasted red peppers, chopped
- 1 (14.5 oz.) can diced tomatoes
- ¼ cup fresh chopped cilantro
- 1 tbsp. lemon juice
- ½ tsp. red pepper flakes
- ½ tsp. black pepper

- Dash cayenne pepper

Instructions:

Heat the oil in a small saucepan over medium heat and stir in the onion. Cook for 3 to 4 minutes until softened then stir in the red peppers, diced tomatoes, garlic and red pepper flakes. Simmer for 10 minutes. Stir in the lemon juice and cilantro then add the fish. Simmer for 5 to 7 minutes until the fish is opaque then stir in the pepper and cayenne. Serve hot.

Cajun Oyster Stew

Prep Time: 45 minutes

Servings: 6 to 8

Ingredients:

- 6 slices bacon, chopped
- 4 tbsp. coconut oil
- 1 tbsp. minced garlic
- 1 cup chopped onion
- ½ cup chopped celery
- ½ cup green onions, chopped
- 1 quart oysters, liquid reserved
- 3 cups almond milk
- ½ cup chopped parsley
- ½ cup canned coconut milk

- ½ cup almond flour

- ¼ cup dry white wine

- ½ tsp. ground white pepper

- Pinch cayenne pepper

Instructions:

Cook the bacon in a stockpot until crisp then spoon out onto paper towels to drain. Add the coconut oil to the pot and stir in the onions and celery. Cook until softened, about 5 minutes. Stir in the green onions, garlic, white pepper and cayenne. Cook for 1 minute when whisk in the almond flour and cook for 3 minutes. Stir in the wine and the oyster liquid along with the almond milk. Bring to a boil then reduce heat and simmer until thickened, about 5 minutes. Add the oysters and parsley then simmer for 3 minutes. Stir in the bacon and coconut milk and cook 1 minute more before serving.

Lobster Coconut Soup

Prep Time: 25 minutes

Servings: 4

Ingredients:

- 2 cooked lobster tails
- 1 tbsp. coconut oil
- 4 cups seafood stock
- 1 cup coconut milk
- 1 cup sliced mushrooms
- 2 chopped green onions
- 1 tbsp. chopped cilantro
- 2 tbsp. lime juice
- 1 tbsp. lime zest

Instructions:

Scoop the lobster meat from the shell then slice and set aside. Heat the oil in a saucepan over medium heat. Stir in the mushrooms and green onion and cook for 5 minutes. Add the broth and lime zest and bring to a boil. Add the remaining ingredients and cook for 3 to 5 minutes. Serve hot.

Hot and Sour Shrimp Soup

Prep Time: 1 ½ hours

Servings: 4 to 6

Ingredients:

- 1 lbs. raw shrimp, with peel
- 1 tsp. sesame oil
- 8 cups chicken stock
- 2 tsp. fresh grated ginger
- 4 cloves garlic, minced
- 4 shallots, sliced
- 4 Serrano peppers, minced
- ¼ cup fish sauce
- ¼ cup fresh cilantro leaves
- ¼ cup chopped basil leaves

- 1/3 cup fresh lime juice
- 1 tsp. black pepper

Instructions:

Peel the shrimp and reserve the shells. Toss the shrimp in the sesame oil and chill for 1 hour. Combine the chicken stock, garlic and ginger in a stockpot and bring to a boil. Reduce heat and simmer for 35 minutes. Add the shrimp shells and simmer for another 20 minutes. Strain the mixture and discard the solids then return the liquid to the pot and bring to a boil. Reduce heat and add the shallots and Serrano peppers. Simmer for 15 minutes then stir in the fish sauce. Add the shrimp then remove from heat and stir in the remaining ingredients. Let stand until the shrimp is cooked through then serve hot.

Vegetarian Recipes

Sweet Potato Stew

Prep Time: 1 hour

Servings: 6

Ingredients:

- 2 lbs. sweet potatoes, chopped
- 1 tbsp. olive oil
- 1 tsp. minced garlic
- 1 cup sliced carrots
- 1 cup sliced celery
- 1 onion, chopped
- 2 cups vegetable broth
- 1 tsp. dried oregano

- ½ tsp. sea salt
- ¼ tsp. pepper

Instructions:

Heat the coconut oil in a Dutch oven over medium heat. Stir in the garlic and cook for 2 minutes. Add the sweet potato and cook until browned, about 5 minutes. Stir in the remaining ingredients and bring to a boil. Reduce heat and simmer, covered, for 45 minutes or until the sweet potatoes are tender.

Butternut Squash Soup

Prep Time: 1 hour

Servings: 4

Ingredients:

- 3 lbs. butternut squash
- 2 tbsp. olive oil
- 1 tsp. minced garlic
- 1 onion, diced
- ½ tsp. nutmeg
- ½ tsp. sea salt
- ¼ tsp. pepper
- 6 cups chicken stock

Instructions:

Peel the squash and cut them in half. Scoop out the seeds and chop the flesh into 1-inch chunks. Heat the oil in a stockpot over medium heat then add the garlic and onions. Cook until the onions are tender, about 10 minutes. Stir in the squash and chicken stock then bring to a boil. Reduce heat and simmer for 25 minutes until the squash is tender. Puree the soup with an immersion blender and season with nutmeg, sea salt and pepper. Serve hot.

Vegetarian Chili

Prep Time: 1 ½ hours

Servings: 4

Ingredients:

- 1 ½ lbs. butternut squash
- 2 ripe avocados, diced
- 2 red peppers, chopped
- 1 red onion, chopped
- 2 tbsp. olive oil
- 1 tbsp. minced garlic
- 1 ½ cups diced tomatoes
- 2 cups vegetable stock
- 1 tbsp. chili powder
- 1 tsp. cumin

- 1 tsp. salt

Instructions:

Peel the squash and cut them in half. Scoop out the seeds and chop the flesh into 1-inch chunks. Heat the oil in a stockpot over medium heat then add the garlic, onion, peppers and squash. Cook for about 15 minutes then stir in the remaining ingredients aside from the avocado. Bring to a boil then reduce heat and simmer, covered, for 1 hour. Serve the chili hot, garnished with diced avocado.

Tomato Basil Soup

Prep Time: 1 hour

Servings: 4

Ingredients:

- 10 large tomatoes, cored and cut in half
- 1 large onion, sliced thin
- 1 tbsp. minced garlic
- 2 tbsp. olive oil
- 1 cup chicken stock
- ½ cup chopped basil leaves
- ½ cup coconut milk
- ½ tsp. white ground pepper

Instructions:

Preheat the oven to 400°F and spread the tomatoes and onions on a baking sheet. Top with garlic and chopped basil then drizzle with olive oil. Roast for 45 minutes, stirring once halfway through. Transfer the vegetables to a stockpot and stir in the chicken stock. Bring to a boil then remove from heat and puree the soup using an immersion blender. Whisk in the coconut milk and pepper then serve hot.

Acorn Squash Soup

Prep Time: 1 ½ hours

Servings: 6 to 8

Ingredients:

- 3 lbs. acorn squash
- ¼ cup olive oil plus 2 tbsp.
- 1 ½ tbsp. minced garlic
- 1 onion, sliced
- 1 tbsp. coconut oil
- 4 cups vegetable broth
- 1 tsp. dried oregano
- ¼ tsp. white pepper
- 1 cup canned coconut milk

Instructions:

Preheat the oven to 350°F and line a baking sheet with foil. Cut the squash in half and scoop out the seeds then lay them on the baking sheet cut-sides up. Top with minced garlic and drizzle with 2 tbsp. olive oil then cook for 45 minutes or until tender. Set aside the squash to cool then scoop the flesh out with a spoon into a bowl. Heat the coconut oil in a stockpot over medium heat. Stir in the squash, onions, broth and spices then bring to a boil. Remove from heat and puree the soup using an immersion blender. Stir in the coconut milk and let sit for 5 minutes before serving.

Pureed Carrot Soup

Prep Time: 1 hour 15 minutes

Servings: 6

Ingredients:

- 3 ½ lbs. carrots, chopped
- 1 tbsp. minced garlic
- 2 tbsp. coconut oil
- 1 tbsp. curry powder
- 1 tsp. sea salt
- ¼ tsp. white ground pepper
- 6 cups vegetable stock

Instructions:

Heat the coconut oil in a large stockpot over medium heat. Stir in the garlic and curry powder and cook for 1 minute. Add the carrots and cook for 25 minutes or until they begin to soften. Whisk in the remaining ingredients and bring to a boil. Reduce heat and simmer for 20 minutes. Remove from heat and blend the soup using an immersion blender. Return to heat and simmer 15 minutes before serving.

Winter Vegetable Stew

Prep Time: 1 hour

Servings: 4

Ingredients:

- 2 tbsp. olive oil
- 1 tsp. minced garlic
- 1 lbs. sweet potatoes, chopped
- 8 oz. baby carrots
- 1 onion, chopped
- 2 turnips, peeled and chopped
- 1 parsnip, peeled and chopped
- 1 ½ cups vegetable stock
- ¼ cup dry white wine
- 1 tsp. dried thyme

- ½ tsp. dried sage

Instructions:

Heat the olive oil in a Dutch oven over medium heat. Stir in the garlic, thyme and sage and cook for 1 minute. Add the carrots, onion, turnips and parsnip then cook for 8 minutes or until the vegetables start to brown. Scoop the vegetables out into a bowl and stir in the white wine. Cook, stirring, until the wine has cooked off. Add the vegetables back to the Dutch oven and stir in the remaining ingredients. Bring to a boil then reduce heat and simmer, covered, for 30 minutes or until the vegetables are tender.

Vegetable Stock

Prep Time: 4 hours

Servings: 1 gallon

Ingredients:

- 1 tbsp. olive oil
- 2 tbsp. minced garlic
- 1 large onion, quartered
- 1 ½ cups chopped carrot
- 1 ½ cups chopped celery
- 2 bay leaves
- 1 bunch green onions
- ½ bunch fresh parsley
- 1 tsp. salt
- 2 quarts water

Instructions:

Heat the olive oil in a large stockpot over medium heat. Add the garlic and cook for 1 minute. Stir in the vegetables and cook for 10 minutes, stirring often. Add the remaining ingredients and bring to a boil. Reduce heat and simmer, uncovered, for 3 hours. Strain the liquid through a mesh sieve and use in your favorite soup recipes.

Creamy Mushroom Soup

Prep Time: 55 minutes

Servings: 4

Ingredients:

- 2 lbs. fresh mushrooms, sliced
- 1 tbsp. coconut oil
- 1 tsp. minced garlic
- 1 onion, chopped
- ¼ cup almond flour
- ½ tsp. white pepper
- ½ cup coconut milk
- 5 cups vegetable stock

Instructions:

Heat the coconut oil in a large saucepan and stir in the garlic.

Cook for 1 minute then add the mushrooms and onions. Cook for 5 minutes until the onions are translucent. Stir in the vegetable stock and bring to a boil. Reduce heat and simmer, covered, for 45 minutes. Whisk together the almond flour and coconut milk then drizzle into the pot while whisking. Season with white pepper and serve hot.

French Onion Soup

Prep Time: 45 minutes

Servings: 4

Ingredients:

- 5 cups beef stock
- 2 tbsp. olive oil
- 3 large onions, sliced thin
- 1 tbsp. minced garlic
- 2 bay leaves
- 1 tbsp. onion powder
- 1 tsp. sea salt
- ½ tsp. black pepper

Instructions:

Heat the coconut oil in a Dutch oven over medium heat. Add

the garlic, salt and pepper and cook for 1 minute. Stir in the onions and cook until softened, about 20 minutes. Whisk in the remaining ingredients and bring to a boil. Reduce heat and simmer for 20 minutes. Discard the bay leaves before serving.

CPSIA information can be obtained at www.ICGtesting.com
Printed in the USA
LVOW04s1939280915

456052LV00026B/625/P